A Light Through the Storm

B. BOYD

ISBN:
ISBN#: 978-1-4566-2100-1

INTRODUCTION

This book is not intended to give you answers on how to fix your child, fix your parenting, or solve your problems. The purpose and goal of this book is simply to relieve your symptoms, validate your feelings, and help you keep your sanity!

That sounds like a simple goal doesn't it? Well, if you are reading this book, you probably realize that it is not so simple. As parents, we all have struggles. Sometimes they are short term and we can weather the storm. Then, there are the times when the storm continues to rage and we begin to lose hope that the light will ever shine again. It is during these times that we need help and hope.

I pray that this book will bring you that help and hope while providing you with ways to care for yourself during these turbulent times. I can remember times, in my own experiences, where I wondered if I could make it through. I became very depressed; I lost hope, felt empty, and helpless.

In each chapter, I will introduce you to "Sanity Savers" that will help you get through this time in your life. Sanity Savers are actions or challenges for you to try in order to help you find relief, hope, and a little bit of light and encouragement. I implore you to step out on faith and try at least one of the Sanity Savers. You would not be reading this book if you had other options or knew what steps to take on your own. It is perfectly understandable to reach out for help, to reach for some type of answer. I have been there myself. My storm was not a brief period of time that I weathered and then quickly recovered. My storm lasted for over 5 years. I felt very much like you. I was at a complete loss, depressed, feeling I was going to have a nervous breakdown, and finding nowhere to turn. The action items included in each chapter, called Sanity Savers, are things that I found helpful in my recovery process. I sincerely hope this book will guide you through your own personal storm and provide you with some small relief, even if it is just to know that you are not alone. We can sometimes feel isolated and think we are alone in dealing with these issues. I cannot tell you how many parents shared their stories with me as I began to open up and share things with other people. Parenting challenges are much more common than we think.

Your storm will have an ending and you will see glimpses of light through the storm. My prayer for you is that your story will have a happy ending and that you will return to the strong, happy person that you once were.

CONTENTS

ACKNOWLEDGMENTS

I want to thank my husband, Neal, for the support and encouragement he gave me in writing this book and getting it across the finish line. I love you and you mean the world to me!

I would like to thank God for all that he has done in my life and for being forever faithful, walking beside down life's path, and carrying me when I was unable to walk on my own.

I want to thank Ruth Bowser for planting the idea of this book in my head.

I want to thank my therapist, Jill Carl, for helping me through one of the most difficult times in my life. Jill you have been a Godsend to me, and I appreciate all you have done to help me in my healing process.

Finally, I want to thank both of my boys. There have been challenging times, but I love them both so dearly, and I would not trade a single moment that I have had with them. I look forward to continuing to watch them grow and change and hope, when I am old and gray, they will love me as much as I have loved them.

1 A LABOR OF LOVE

From the time I was a very young girl, I always wanted to be a mom. I come from a large family of 10. I started babysitting when I was eleven. I babysat for my nieces and nephews and for other kids as well. I loved children and looked forward to the day when I would have my own children. Children are so fun to be around. They are happy and put a smile on your face. A child's laughter is contagious. There could be no greater joy than to be a mom.

I married when I was 20, had my first child when I was 21 and my second at 24. I remember so clearly the incredible feeling of being pregnant and having a child grow within me. A woman glows when she is pregnant. It is an incredible time and a true miracle. Labor with both of my boys was pretty quick, and I had both of them naturally with no pain medication. Giving birth was a physically painful experience but as soon as you see your beautiful baby, you soon forget all of the pain because you are filled with an overwhelming love for this new life that you brought into the world. In Psalm 127:3-5 it says, "Don't you see that children are God's best gift? The fruit of the womb his generous legacy? Like a warrior's fistful of arrows are the children of a vigorous youth. Oh, how blessed are you parents, with your quivers full of children!" *MSG* Being a parent is a true blessing but it is also the most difficult job that you will ever do.

I truly enjoyed parenting my children as they grew. We went to Disney World when they were 5 and 2. Both of my boys starting playing soccer when they were 4. They played soccer, baseball, football, and roller hockey. It was a busy time but a joyful one as well. I think I was as competitive as they were. As my boys became pre-teens and teens, things started to change. They were growing more independent and starting to make decisions on their own. I thought I had taught them well. We talked about everything and I provided sound instruction to them.

As time passed and they became older, I discovered them starting to make decisions that I didn't approve of. We sat down and talked about their decisions. I warned them of possible consequences based on my own experiences. Unfortunately, neither of my children were willing to learn from me. They wanted to learn the hard way, through their own experience. All of the sudden I found myself in brand new territory. What I thought would work was no longer working. The children I adored, I started to despise. I found myself in a love/hate relationship with them. I recently heard a sermon at church where the minister discussed love and asked the church, "What is the opposite of love?" My minister described how the opposite of love is not hate. Love and hate are closely related and are very strong emotions that often go together. The opposite of love is not hate, it is apathy. Apathy is not feeling anything, not caring. If you have picked up this book, then I know you love your children. You may also be in a love/hate relationship with your children. That is okay, it is much better to be there, than to feel apathy for your children.

Have you ever stopped and thought about LOVE? What is love? Why is it such a strong emotion? How can it feel so good at times and cause us so much hurt at others? The dictionary defines love as "a feeling of warm personal attachment or deep affection, as for a parent, child, or friend."

Love is so complex that the one English word is not enough to truly describe all of its facets. In Greek, there are four different words for love: Eros, Philia, Agape, and Storge. Eros is passionate love felt between a man and a woman used to describe romantic love. Philia means friendship in modern day Greek and is characterized by loyalty between friends, family, community and can also be used to express the love for an activity. Agape love means "I love you". It denotes feelings for one's child or spouse and is illustrated by a self-sacrificing and giving love to all. Storge means "affection", like that felt by parents for their offspring.

The love between a parent and their child is an extremely powerful love that encompasses Philia, Agape, and Storge kinds of love. We (with the power of God) created that life. They are our flesh and blood. We have a special bond with them. The love is so strong that we would do anything for our child. As parents, we will do anything to protect them, to keep them from harm, and ensure their safety. Throughout history parents have done incredible things for their children in the name of love. Mothers have been known to have super powers when their child is in a dangerous situation and lift a car, run into a burning building, and leap buildings in a single bound (okay maybe that one is Superman). We may have even lied for our children or defended them even when others have solid accusations against them. We think, there is no way "my child" could do something like that. Some parents have also had to make hard decisions in the name of love. Examples include giving up a child for adoption so they can have a better life than we can provide or turning them into the authorities when they have done something terribly wrong. Love is hard. It is the most incredible feeling in the world. It can also be the most heart wrenching thing in the world, especially when the love we give is not returned to us.

Love is a gift and each of us has a desire to give and receive it, which is why it is so ironic how love can be used and abused. Often times, the people we love the most are the same people that we hurt the most. Doesn't that seem strange? Why do we as human beings do that? It is because we feel safe with those who love us. We are family. We have something in our brains that tells us, this person will always love me, always be there for me…no matter what I do. For the most part that is true. We put up with more abuse from those we love than we would from friends, co-workers or strangers. Our children know us well. They have been around us their whole lives. They know what buttons to push, how to gain our sympathy, how to irritate us, how to wear us down AND they use it against us.

We often treat people we love in ways that we would never treat others. We accept treatment from those we love that we would never take from others. This is why it is so difficult for us as parents. We love our children. We want them to be happy and successful. We want what is best for them. We want to protect them. Unfortunately, as our children grow up, they make their own decisions. Sometimes they make good decisions and sometimes they make bad ones. We want to protect them from the bad decisions but they won't let us. Sometimes they need to learn the hard way; not from our wisdom or experience, but from their own.

The Bible teaches us about unconditional love. God has this unconditional love for us. God is faithful to us even when we are not faithful. Unconditional love is very difficult to acquire and to practice in our lives on a daily basis. We get angry with others, feel hurt, feel betrayed, and a mired of other feelings. It is difficult to practice unconditional love especially with our spouses. We have lines, draw boundaries and if someone crosses those lines, it is often the end of the relationship. The strange thing is, that even though we can sometimes do this so easily with a spouse, it is much harder with our children. My heart has been broken and torn apart from things that my child has done. I felt hatred in my heart towards my child at times, but I still love him no matter what. I worry about him. I would give anything to help him. No matter what the cost, if my child needs me, I will be there for him. When we become parents and go through trials with our children, it is easier to understand how God feels about us. The Bible teaches us to hate the sin but love the sinner. Sometimes it can be hard to separate the two.

We have to be careful with our love for our children because it can easily cloud our judgment. Proverbs 10:12 says, "...love covers all wrongs", but be careful that you don't love them so much that you excuse their behavior. Sometimes tough love is what is needed. It is easy to fall into the trap of becoming an enabler. Allowing others to depend on us too much or to take advantage of us does not help them in the end. Instead it prolongs the dependencies and stunts the ability for our children to grow and learn to accept the consequences of their actions.

As parents, we need to set boundaries. Boundaries define what is acceptable and what is not; what is right and what is wrong. Boundaries provide security for our children. They provide a sense of order in what can sometimes be chaos. Sometimes the boundaries work, but there are times that they may not. Picture yourself standing in an open area. You and your children are together and you draw a line in the dirt. At some point, usually when our children are teenagers, they move closer to the line. They may occasionally cross it but then return to the boundary inside the line. Then, as most of you are probably experiencing, you find yourself on one side of the line and your child is on the other. Each time the line is crossed, a new line is drawn. You are choosing your battles; you are beginning to make compromises. You are comparing your child to the world. You are saying in your mind, "Well, it could be worse, he could be doing X". There is suddenly a new line and then another new line. The line is getting wider and wider and has grown far away from the original line. Storms come and begin digging a deeper rut in the line that has been created. Soon the line is a trench. Eventually, the line is no longer a line but a deep cavern that separates you from your child. It is at this time that you are at a loss. What do I do? How can I get my child to come back across the line to the side that is safe? The place where I can protect my child, see what he or she is doing, and be able to reach them.

It is possible that your child doesn't want to come back to the safe side inside the line. Over time that gap between you and them grows deeper and wider. Don't give up hope, there is still a way to reach them. It may take a lot of work and a lot of time, but there is hope. You can build a bridge across the divide. We will talk about this more in chapter 12 where we discuss re-building.

So what do you do when you are filled with love for your child and you find yourself in a place where the love is not returned or your love doesn't seem like enough? Try one or all of the Sanity Savers listed below.

Sanity Savers

Sanity Savers:

1. Read the book <u>Boundaries with Teens</u> by Henry Cloud and John Townsend

2. Love yourself first and foremost

3. Make your relationship with your loved one about more than just the current issue or problem

4. Share your love with someone who is receptive to it

1. **Read the book <u>Boundaries</u> by Henry Cloud and John Townsend or <u>Boundaries with Teens</u>**
   - ❖ Loving your children does not mean giving them everything they want or need. Sometimes loving them means telling them "No" and not enabling them. Make

them accept responsibility for their actions and suffer the consequences.

❖ We cannot always rescue them. Kids need to learn their own lessons and feel pain in order to learn not to repeat the same pattern.

2. **Love yourself first and foremost.**
   ❖ Treat yourself with the respect that you deserve. Don't allow yourself to be treated poorly. We have the ability to decide how we should be treated. Tell others what is acceptable and what is not.

   ❖ Do something for you. Make sure that you take time to do something that you enjoy and allow yourself time to re-energize. You are no help to anyone if you are worn down and unable to think clearly or function fully.

3. **Make your relationship with your loved one about more than just the current issue or problem.**
   ❖ When there is turmoil in a relationship, it is easy to focus on what needs to be fixed, talk about the problems, and remind them what needs to be done or changed. If this is all that you do, it will tear down the relationship and push your loved one away.

   ❖ Remember the things you love about the person. Go do something fun with them. Spend time laughing, playing, whatever you can think of other than focusing on the problem. This will strengthen the relationship and give both parties a break from what is going on and hopefully be a catalyst to move past the problems.

4. Share your love with someone who is receptive to it.

❖ Find another outlet where you can give love and feel good about what you are doing. Serve at a shelter, babysit for someone, or brighten someone's day with a note, card, email, or phone call.

❖ The parent/child relationship is very important and is going to require a great deal of patience, love and nurturing. However, by serving others and seeing others in need will help you put things in perspective. Yes, your situation is bad but it can always be worse. This is in no way intended to diminish your pain or your circumstances. It is meant to let you know that you are not alone. Everyone has issues of one kind or another. God intends for us to be united and turn to him in prayer. Trusting God will be your greatest sanity.

❖ Go on a special date with your spouse or hang out with a good friend. Don't talk about the problems while on the date.

2 MANAGE THE STRESS

Stress is a funny thing. It starts out small and before you know it, it is this huge monster weighing you down. There have been many times when I didn't think I was stressed in my mind (you know when you tell yourself that you have it under control and you shouldn't be stressed), but my body says something completely different. All of the signs are there. Sometimes we don't see them very clearly, but the people around us do.

Stress is a powerful force that affects us in more ways than we know or can imagine. Prolonged stress can take a serious toll on our bodies. It is the body's way of telling us it's time to stop, slow, take a break, or get some help. Let's talk about two types of stress: Acute Stress (short-term) that results from a stressful event and Chronic Stress (long-term) which is characterized by stressful circumstances or problems. Acute stress has a specific start and end. It is your body's instant response to any situation that is dangerous or demanding. An example of acute stress would be something like an automobile accident, a deadline on a project at work, or skiing down a steep mountain or challenging run (like a black diamond). It can be exciting and thrilling and is short term with little impact to our health.

Chronic stress is something completely different. Chronic stress is the grinding stress that wears you down, day after day, year after year. It can be described as never-ending trouble. There is no end in sight and you begin to feel hopeless. Examples of chronic stress could include money problems, an unhappy marriage, a dysfunctional family, a chronic disease...or in the case this book focuses on, a troubled teen that we, as parents, seem unable to reach.

Being a parent is so challenging. I don't remember my mom having such a hard time when I was growing up. Maybe things have changed, or maybe I only remember what I want to remember. I think it is a combination of both. Our world is a scary place, and our kids are exposed to far more temptations then we experienced, some of which can be very dangerous. I grew up in a small town in Iowa. There was little traffic and nowhere to really go. Drugs weren't a part of the school, and it wasn't popular to use them. My teenage years were far different than what my kids experienced, and I would definitely say that I was very naive. I have two boys. They have both graduated high school (thank God). Both of them began to struggle in their Junior year of high school. You know how they say that your kids are very different because you couldn't handle two children with the same character? Well, mine both have very different personalities, but they both started out with the same struggles their junior year of high school. My oldest, Jay, started smoking pot, sneaking out of the house, taking the car without asking, failing classes, and all of those fun things that teenagers do.

I was incredibly stressed. I was frustrated that he wouldn't listen and that I had to babysit him every night to do his homework. I couldn't trust what he told me. One day, I got a call from the school. He arrived at school high from smoking marijuana. The police officer at the school searched his car and found a pipe with residue in it. They charged him with drug possession and possession of drug paraphernalia. This news horrified me. This couldn't be my child. We were a church going family. Not just on the holidays, but every Sunday. My children were raised in the church, they knew right from wrong.

Jay was suspended from school and had to attend drug and alcohol classes. The class required the teens to attend with their parents. I didn't mind attending the 2 hour classes for 8 weeks, but I wondered why I was being forced to attend a class because of what my son had done. That sounds bad, and I don't mean it that way. The point I am trying to make is that our children's actions affect us even when we don't want them to. I am a parent that clearly understands the effects and consequences of drug and alcohol use and taught this to my children. However, I did learn a lot in the classes. I tried again to re-enforce those teachings with Jay, but he felt he was smarter than me or the instructor. He proceeded to explain to me that she did not know what she was talking about. Those side effects and consequences that she described, don't really happen to people who smoke. Clearly Jay, at the young age of 17, knew far more than me and the instructor.

During the trials with Jay, I began to feel very angry. I was angry that Jay wasn't following the rules, angry that he was making such bad choices, and most of all I was angry that I couldn't make him change. I tried. I talked with him, I reasoned with him, I explained the side effects, and the consequences. I tried to give him a vision of the future that poor choices create versus the future he wanted. I couldn't get through. This was the beginning of the 5 stages of grief. I would go through all of them with Jay and my other son, Steve.

At the time Jay started down this path, I was a single mom. His dad was serving in the military over in Iraq. I was alone, embarrassed and frustrated. I felt I couldn't turn to my friends because I didn't want them to know what was happening. I am a Christian and having people know that my child was smoking pot seemed far too embarrassing. I felt I would be judged and people might looked down on me. It felt like one of those secrets that you never tell anyone. At least that is how I felt initially.

As Jay started down this path, Steve, his younger brother, saw the effects. He saw how it hurt me. He saw the fear that I had. He saw the stress I was going through. I thought that he would learn from what Jay did and not venture down the same path. Unfortunately, I was very wrong about that. Not only did he start down the same path, but he experimented with far more things than Jay had. He began experimenting with various kinds of drugs, got involved with some really bad people, and found himself in a lot of costly legal trouble.

I spent 5+ years in an extended period of chronic stress. It started out with the usual symptoms of stress. I was emotionally spent. I felt tired and drained. Over time, the stress continued to get worse. I couldn't sleep at night. I started having stomach problems. My digestive system was not functioning properly and eating made me feel worse. My back and neck were extremely tense. I was in constant pain from the stress in my shoulders and neck. I also felt a tremendous sense of guilt. I often wondered what I had done wrong. I asked myself daily, "How could this have happened?" I often cried myself to sleep at night. Then I started getting severe migraine headaches. I was a huge mess.

I got Eczema for the first time in my life. This may or may not be related to stress, but it is very strange for it to manifest for the first time in someone who is in their 40s. I had a hard time concentrating. The things that I used to love were no longer enjoyable for me.

I tried everything possible to get help for my children and for myself. In this book, I focus on help for the parents, so I will not go into the details of finding help for our children. However, I will provide some resources at the end of the book that may be helpful for you.

As you read through the Sanity Savers in each Chapter, you will see the various things I tried in my effort to minimize the stress and emotions that I felt. Some worked better than others and I will share what worked best for me. However, what worked for me may not work for you. It doesn't hurt to try all of the ideas or create some of your own. Find what works best for you and keep moving down that path until you get past this storm in your life and begin to see the light break through.

Be patient with yourself and with your efforts to get healthier because none of the Sanity Savers are going to be a quick fix. It will take time for you to feel better. Tough situations in our lives can take an extreme toll on us both physically and emotionally. It is important to learn to manage the stress early on so that it does not manifest itself into something really serious. I waited too long to get the help I needed. I sincerely hope that you will not do the same.

Sanity Savers

Sanity Savers:

1. Exercise
2. Massage
3. Acupuncture
4. Begin to journal

1. **Exercise**

   ❖ Exercise will make you feel better so even when you don't feel like working out, push yourself to do even a short work out. Trust me, it will make you feel better. Try something that you will enjoy so it doesn't feel like work. Yoga is a great way to stretch your muscles. It teaches breathing and relaxation techniques that are useful when dealing with stressful situations.

   ❖ "Exercise essentially burns away the chemicals like cortisol and norepinephrine that cause stress. At the same time, vigorous exercise releases endorphins into the system. Endorphins are morphine-like hormones that are responsible for the feeling of elation, or well-being that distance runners get from running. Other chemicals like dopamine and serotonin are also released in the brain during exercise. Together, these give a feeling of safety and security that contributes to off-setting some of the "internal" causes of stress, such as uncertainty, pessimism and negative self-talk."
   Learn more:
   http://www.naturalnews.com/028727_exercise_anxiety.html#ixzz2TzJ5rEG2

2. **Massage**

   ❖ "Massage therapy is a proven, non-invasive way to reduce chronic stress levels in the body. Dozens of studies have shown the effectiveness of massage

therapy in reducing stress and millions of people avail themselves to the services of massage therapists to treat stress. Using massage to reduce stress is natural and safe and unlike some forms of alternative therapies, massage therapy is a proven discipline within the medical community with scientific evidence supporting the use of massage for stress management."
http://massageadvancer.com/studies-conclusively-show-massage-therapy-reduces-stress/277

3. **Acupuncture**

   ❖ There are several ways that acupuncture reduces stress and its side-effects. The first is that acupuncture is very relaxing. Once the needles are inserted, you lie on a massage table and rest for 15-30 minutes. The lights are low and soft music plays and many patients fall into a state of deep and total relaxation. After treatment, many people feel calm and at the same time restored to their more natural self. Secondly, while you are resting, the acupuncture needles are working to balance your whole body. For instance, if, because of stress, you experience chronic neck and shoulder pain, the treatment will focus on relaxing muscle tension and increasing circulation to tight, ischemic areas. Or, if your reaction to stress is more emotional, treatments will help to balance mood swings and release pent-up feelings. If your health is beginning to suffer because of stress and disease is occurring, acupuncture can treat and reduce or eliminate the problem (see specific disease conditions on this site to understand how acupuncture treats these problems). Long term stress may manifest in many different symptoms occurring at the same time. Acupuncture helps to address the origin of the problem, while at the same time reducing the painful symptoms that are affecting your health and well-being.

http://triangleacupunctureclinic.com/learn/emotional/stress

❖ I found acupuncture to be the most helpful for me in dealing with stress and the physical and emotional turmoil that I experienced.

4. **Journaling**

❖ If you don't have anyone to confide in or are afraid to share what is going on with others, then journaling is wonderful. It gives you an outlet for expressing your feelings. It gets things out of your head so you are not replaying them over and over again. The best medicine is getting everything out so you don't feel the built up pressure and instead can release it. By writing things down, it may actually help you sleep and provide you a sense of peace. Journaling can be very therapeutic. The best part is that it only takes a pen and a piece of paper. It is the least expensive form of therapy that you will find. One father who had two sons that were addicted to drugs wrote in a journal throughout his entire ordeal and later published it in the hope of helping other parents.

❖ The wonderful thing about journaling is that it can be your very own private feelings and thoughts, and it is entirely up to you whether or not you share that with anyone. What you write is for you alone. You do not need to share it with anyone else unless you want to share it. If you are at a loss for how to deal with life and what is going on, I encourage you start by writing down your thoughts, feelings, and experiences.

3 YOU'RE NOT MY CHILD (SHAME / EMBARRASSMENT)

How do you introduce yourself to others? Hi, my name is Sue and I am a student, architect, lawyer, doctor, student, home maker OR I am so and so's Daughter, Sister, Wife, Mother, etc. All too often our identities are caught up in what we do or what role we play rather than who we are. Those jobs and roles are a part of who we are but they don't describe our character, ethics, morals, values, passions, missions, or how we handle situations life throws at us. We easily dismiss our character traits and instead gain so much of our worth and value from what we have accomplished or what we do for a living. If we can't produce what we want or what we think is expected of us, then we view ourselves as failures. Not only do we view ourselves that way, we believe others see us the same way.

As a parent, our identity is often caught up in our children and what they do or don't do. We are proud when they show great athleticism. We brag about how good they are and the talent they have. We get "credit" for their accomplishments as if we had something to do with it. We gave them birth and they have our genes. Unfortunately, the same is true when our children display poor behavior. Parents of a murderer are looked upon as the monsters their children have become. Most people feel like the parents should have known and done something to prevent the incident or actions of their children. Let me say, no one dreams that one day their child will be a murderer, a drug addict, an alcoholic, a bully, or a criminal. When our children take a path less desired, we are devastated. This is not how we raised our children to be. It is not the plan we had for their lives. It is not the path we chose for them or the direction in which we lead them. Somehow...it just happened. Sometimes there are signs and we try to course correct when we see those signs. Sometimes that course correction doesn't work. There is a certain age when our children begin to make their own decisions. Their decisions are not based on what their parents would do or what their parents would advise, they are based upon the independent minded young adults they want to become. They are based on what their peers are doing. They are based on a misguided sense of adventure or excitement.

Around the age of 17, both of my boys started down this path of independence and began to make mistakes that would impact their lives and mine. I don't know why or how it happened, but it did. Jay mad some decisions that seemed bad at the time, but were minor in comparison to what I would face with Steve. My husband believes that peer pressure plays a huge part in the choices that teens make. I am not certain what brought about the changes and choices but it was the beginning of a long road for me. That road would bring me on a journey that would alter the person that I am and leave me searching for the person that I would become.

It all started around the time that Jay was 17. He had started acting out and rebelling as a teenager. It was so out of character for him and our family. One night, I was out with a friend and her husband. I started talking about how Jay's grades were slipping in school and that he was sneaking out of the house. My friend's husband said, "I bet he is smoking pot". I was positive he was wrong. That is not happening. My son would never do that. We had talked about drugs and the dangers. I believed Jay was too smart to get involved with anything that would harm his body or mental faculties. I was so naive. As I found out later, that was exactly what he was doing. I was upset. I could not believe that my child would do smoke marijuana. I talked to Jay, told him to stop, but he continued down this path. One day, it had all built up and I had enough. I told him to get out if he couldn't obey my rules. He did. He left and I didn't know where he was for a few days. He had been staying with a friend who lived a few blocks from us. He was still attending school each day so I waited to see how things would play out.

About a week later, I was sitting at work and got a phone call. It was from the security guard at the local grocery store. He told me that my son had been caught shoplifting. He said I could come down and pick him up if Jay agreed to pay restitution. If I didn't want to do that, then he would call the police and Jay would get charged. I honestly didn't know what to do. I had never been faced with anything like this. I called Jay's father, Jim. We had gotten divorced a few years earlier. He did not answer his phone. This wasn't unusual. Jim left most of the parenting to me. He and Jay didn't have much of a relationship at all. I remember feeling so upset and not knowing what the right thing to do would be. Who could I turn to?

I had a friend whose husband was a police officer so I decided to give him a call and get some advice. He didn't answer either. Next I called my ex-husband's wife to see where Jim was. She answered and told me that he was out golfing. I told her it was urgent and I needed to speak with him. She would try and get in touch with him and have him call me. I got in the car and started heading from work to the grocery store. On the drive, Jim called me. I explained the situation and asked Jim what I should do. He simply said, "I don't care, let him go to jail". That was it, end of conversation and he had hung up so he could get back to his golf game.

What now? I understood sin and consequences, and I was not opposed to making my child suffer the consequences, but at the same time this was my son. I was scared for him and I didn't know what would happen. He needed to learn a lesson and maybe this was the opportunity. Just then, my friend, the police officer, called me. I explained the situation and asked him what would happen if I had the store call the police. He said they would take him to the police station and then call me to come pick him up. I would have to pay court costs and the whole nine yards, but they would not keep him overnight or send him to juvenile detention. In my mind this translated into me being inconvenienced and having to pay a bunch of money and Jay would still not learn any lessons. Based on that, I decided to go pick him up from the grocery store and have him pay the restitution.

When I arrived at the store, Jay was sitting in the security room. I was angry that my son would do this. He has had stolen a candy bar and some condoms totaling $7.50. The restitution cost was $250. I started interrogating him. Why would you do this, what were you thinking? That is when I saw his eyes. He was clearly high. That made me even angrier. What is wrong with you?!? We finished the paperwork and left the store. We got in the car and headed home. I was yelling at him the entire way home, and he sat there and acted like he didn't care or that it was no big deal. When we pulled in the garage, I reached over and hit him in the chest to try and get his attention and wake him up to what he had done. I got out of the car and went around to go in the house. I had pushed things too far. Jay grabbed me out of anger and started throwing me against the side of the garage. We were physically fighting for the first time in our lives. Jay's step-dad heard us and came running out to the garage. Just then, Jay threw me a second time into the wall and I swung and hit the side of his head. My husband grabbed him off me, and we went into the house and called the police.

The police arrived and we described what happened. My hand was throbbing and they asked if I wanted them to call an ambulance. I said no. They asked if I wanted to press charges against Jay. The consequences would be the same again. Court costs, fees, etc. but no time in jail for my son. I said no.

That episode was a horrible time and I am not proud of how I handled it. My hand ended up being broken and I had to deal with questions for six weeks about how I broke my hand. I could not bring myself to tell anyone that I had hit my son. Although many people asked jokingly if I had hit my husband or my kids. Little did they know. Not only was I ashamed of what my son had done, now I was ashamed of what I had done.

I was ashamed when I was called to the school and found out my son Jay had arrived high on marijuana. I was embarrassed when he stole from a store. I was devastated when I found out my son, Steve, was using cocaine. I hid what was happening in my home from everyone I knew. I was terrified to tell anyone. How could this have happened to me and to my children? That is not how I raised my children. We were a middle class family. My children were not spoiled. They were taught to respect people, to follow the rules, and to be good, upstanding citizens. What had happened? How could this be? What would I do?

When our lives and the lives of our children don't turn out the way we plan or hope, we take it very personally. We are ashamed. We feel like a failure and we don't want anyone to know about it. We isolate ourselves; hide what is going on because we are embarrassed and don't want anyone to know the truth. We are afraid of what people will think of us. Sounds a little crazy, doesn't it. Well, it is not so crazy after all. Consider how many times you have been at a store or in a restaurant and seen a child behaving badly. What is your first thought? Something like, "Where is their mother?", "What is wrong with that mother?", "If that were my child, I would...". We are quick to judge, quick to criticize. We have no idea what is going on with that family or situation. We have no idea what has been done to try and correct the behavior. We have no idea what the parents are going through or what other dynamics they are dealing with in life, yet we still judge!

No one wants to be judged in that way. That fear of judgment is what keeps us in isolation, alone with nowhere to turn for help, or at least that is how we feel. I felt this way for so long, and it tore me up inside. I kept all of these feelings inside and didn't share them with anyone. I got to the point where I could no longer handle the stress and the sadness. Finally, I opened up to a group of women from a Bible study that I was leading. I was shocked to find that not one person there judged me. They were grateful that I shared my situation with them. They began to pray for my sons and my family. I felt a sense of freedom for the first time in a long time. We need to remember that the only one who can judge us is God, the one who judges justly. Here are some scriptures that will help with this:

- John 8:15 – "You judge by human standards; I pass judgment on no one."
- John 7:24 – "Stop judging by mere appearances, but instead judge correctly."
- Ephesians 3:12 – "In him and through faith in him we may approach God with freedom and confidence."

The only place that shame gets us is in isolation, feeling sorry for ourselves, afraid, and alone. We feel that our children's actions reflect poorly on us and we are to blame for what has happened or what is going wrong. Remember that no one is perfect. We are all human and we all make mistakes. No one has ever been a perfect parent except God, the Father.

The other thing that we need to remember is that we are given the freedom of choice. We all choose our own path. We can choose to accept the situations that life has given us or we can choose to be victims. This is true for us and for our children. We don't have the ability to change anyone except ourselves. So don't blame yourself and certainly don't let your child blame you for what is happening. You did not hold that cigarette to their mouth and make them smoke it. You did not give them those drugs, or that drink. You did not teach them to steal, to lie, or to cheat. Whatever the situation, it is not your fault. You did the best that you could. We will talk more about this in the next chapter.

There are many arguments around nature vs. nurture and what impacts a child's psyche. In recent studies, some psychologists believe that a child's character is formed as early as 3 years of age and is a good predictor of the kind of adults they will become. Did you feel like you could control your child's behavior, character, and actions at the age of 3? Imagine trying at 16, 17, or 18.   The Bible tells us in Proverbs 22:6, "Teach a child in the way he should go and when he is old he will not stray from it." That is a beautiful thought, and I wish it worked out that way every time. Unfortunately, it doesn't or at least not in my situation. I felt I had taught my children how to make good decisions, live the right way, and be a good person. They had a good foundation and a loving home that would allow them to grow and flourish. They had the ability to become anything they wanted to be. What they wanted to be was free to experiment and make their own choices. That is exactly what they did. They did what they wanted, or what they thought they wanted, at the time. There was nothing I could do to change it. The choices they made embarrassed me and left me sad and distrait.

Sanity Savers

> ### Sanity Savers:
>
> 1. **Find a confidant**
> 2. **Document 3 Great Things about yourself**
> 3. **Memorize Philippians 4:13**

1. **Find someone to confide in.**
   - ❖ Talk to a friend, talk to a family member, talk to a counselor, or a pastor. Depending on your situation, it might be better to choose someone other than a family member if they are judgmental. The more you open up about what is going on, the better you will feel. You will realize that you are not alone, and everyone has problems of one kind or another to deal with and there is no reason to be ashamed.

2. **Write down three great things about yourself and post them where you can see them every day.**
    - ❖ Practice positive self-talk. This will help you feel more confident and remind you that you are a good person. The daily reminder will be helpful to move past the shame and embarrassment and move you toward feeling confident in your abilities as a parent.

    - ❖ God loves you and has forgiven your sins. Don't continue to crucify yourself, Christ already did that for you.

3. **Memorize Philippians 4:13.**

    - ❖ Philippians 4:13 says, "I can do all things through him who gives me strength." God will give you strength to get through your difficult times in life. Lean on Him, trust Him, and you will find help and healing.

4 THE BLAME GAME (GUILT)

I remember waking up each day, getting ready for work and then heading out to start my day. I felt like this big, dark cloud hung over me. It was like a weight, constantly on my shoulders. Whenever I had a moment to think, I would be overcome with a sense of guilt. What had happened? What had I done wrong? What did I not do that I should have done? These were the only thoughts that played over and over again in my head. It was my fault. Somehow, I had failed my children. Maybe it was the divorce. I didn't want the divorce and I couldn't predict or prevent my husband from falling in love with another women. Even though these events were out of my control, I still felt it was my fault.

I stopped forcing my children to go to church when they decided they no longer wanted to attend. I didn't meet every kid they decided to hang out with. I didn't monitor their every action. I knew logically that I could not monitor them 24/7, but still, my brain and my heart kept telling me that somehow it was my fault. I thought I had raised them right and I thought that I was a good parent. I viewed parenting like an arithmetic problem, 1+1=2, but it did not add up that way for me. I thought if you followed the formula, everything would turn out the way it is supposed to. I am a perfectionist by nature. I was very conscientious and I did the right things at the right times. I made logical choices. I taught my children about life and how to navigate through it. I provided them with plans and ideals on how to be successful. Something had gone terribly wrong though. What was happening? This is not what I planned. My world had been turned upside down. The only place that I could look was inside of me. I was consumed with guilt. It slowly ate away at me, day after day. The stress got worse. My body ached. I started having severe headaches that just wouldn't go away. I couldn't talk about my children without crying.

I don't really remember how long this went on, but eventually, I sought some help. I started going to a therapist that a woman from church had recommended. She immediately recommended that I start taking anti-depressants. At the time, I refused, thinking that I would be okay and could manage. Then she started pushing me to send my son, Steve, away to a facility for addicts and kids with behavior problems. I did check into one of the places she recommended, but it did not seem like the right thing at the time and I didn't have the resources to afford it.

I started taking my son, Steve, to a therapist. His dad was in Afghanistan at the time and I was trying my best to get him some help. Steve didn't like the therapist so I decided to bring him to see the therapist I was seeing. They hit it off and Steve enjoyed going to see her each week. I stopped seeing the therapist when she started telling me what Steve shared with her but said I couldn't talk to him about it or ask him about it because it would make her lose her credibility with him. The therapist behavior was unethical but I allowed him to continue seeing her because I wanted to get help for him. He continued to see her for some time but nothing in his behavior changed. Things progressively got worse. Steve started blaming me, his dad, and his brother for his problems. It was our fault. It was my fault he was no longer going to go to college after high school. It was his brother's fault that he tried marijuana for the first time. He couldn't or wouldn't take any of the blame himself.

As a society, we are constantly looking for someone to blame for all of our problems. The government doesn't provide proper health care, taxes are too high, I can't afford an education, my employer doesn't pay enough or provide good benefits, my husband is disengaged and moody and that is why my life is awful…the list goes on and on. There is always someone to blame when things in our life don't go the way we planned. We often play the victim, or people make us out to be the victim. It is not healthy to go through life blaming others. Each of us needs to take a look at ourselves, accept responsibility, and then make good choices about how we want to change and move forward. There are some people in life, though, who will never accept the responsibility. Those people are hard to deal with and we can only hope that one day they will see the light and change. If they don't, we have to decide whether or not to continue our relationship. One must choose to accept the way they are or separate ourselves from them.

The key you need to remember and hold on to is to not let anyone blame you for the choices they have made. It is not yours to own. Each one of us has free will to choose the path we take. There are so many people in the world who did not experience good, supportive parents, but they still manage to have successful lives. There are others who grew up in extreme poverty, but have taken those life experiences and made a better way for themselves. It takes a strong person to do that, but the possibility is within each of us, we just have to have the desire to make the change.

I know that I have made mistakes with my children and I am willing to take ownership of them. I cannot change what is in the past, I can only start from this point forward and try my best to make the best of each situation as it comes up. There will be events that are out of my sphere of influence. I, like you, can only own what is mine and let the rest go. I will also make my children own the decisions and mistakes that are theirs. I cannot and should not accept the blame for the choices that they have made.

If you have made mistakes like me and are feeling guilty, you need to stop. It will not change anything, it won't make you feel better and it certainly will not help your loved one if you accept the blame. Free yourself of the guilt. Try one of these sanity savers.

Sanity Savers

Sanity Savers:

1. Avoid being Manipulated
2. Forgive Yourself
3. Re-program your Thinking (Positive Self-Talk)

1. **Avoid being Manipulated**
    ❖ Manipulation is a behavior a person may use in order to get their way. They may say certain things or behave in a certain way as to make someone give them what they want. Generally, in this situation, what they want is to push the blame onto someone else so they don't have to accept responsibility. Accepting responsibility means admitting that they have a problem and they need to do something to fix that problem. Your child may not be ready for that step and so they will continue to manipulate and blame you; the problem is then you and not them.

    ❖ To avoid being manipulated, try some of these steps:
    ● Calmly explain that you are not willing to accept the blame. Everyone needs to accept responsibility for their own actions. No one forced them to do what they have done or make the choices they have made.

- You may need to distance yourself.

- Work on building your confidence so you stop allowing yourself to be manipulated. You know the truth and what you have done. Even if you have made mistakes, that does not mean you are responsible for what someone else does.

- Stop being fearful. If you can eliminate the fear, it can no longer be used to manipulate you into feeling guilty. Children will manipulate you and try to get you to accept responsibility for their actions.

2. Forgive Yourself

❖ You must forgive yourself in order to let go of the feeling of guilt or remorse. We are responsible for our own emotions and our actions. Re-train your mind to know that what you were in the past is not who you are in the present. You may have made mistakes in the past, but you cannot go back and change what has happened. Where are you today? If you are accepting responsibility, being the best that you can be, and seeking help for what you want to change, then that is the best you can do. Let the past stay in the past. Move forward into the future...guilt free.

3. Re-program your Thinking (Positive Self-Talk)

❖ Positive self-talk is a great way to improve your self-esteem. All too often we talk to ourselves in a negative tone. Instead of entertaining these negative thoughts, replace them with positive ones. Every time you begin to think something negative, turn that around into a positive thought. For example, when your son is late coming home, instead of worrying that something bad has happened, think a positive thought that he is out having a good time and lost track of time. Or maybe he drove a friend home because that friend shouldn't have been driving, and he will be home soon. Write positive statements on sticky notes or note cards and put them in places that you can see throughout the day. Some examples of positive self-talk includes: "I am a strong person", "I can handle anything", "I am worthy of respect", "I will have a great day today", "I will be fear free today", "I am a beautiful person", etc.

5 WHAT CAN I DO? (HELPLESSNESS)

I awoke with a start and had this overwhelming sense that something was terribly wrong. I glanced over at the clock in my bedroom and saw that it was 2:00 am. I had no idea why I woke up so abruptly. I didn't recall dreaming about anything. I felt the Holy Spirit had awaken me to warn me something was wrong, I just wasn't sure what that thing was. I had this sense of dread. I couldn't shake it and was unable to go back to sleep. I lay there for the next few hours tossing and turning, trying to go back to sleep. As soon as my alarm went off, I got up and went to my son Steve's room. It was nearly time for him to get up for school. I crawled in his bed and lay down beside him. I told him that I was woken in the middle of the night with a strong sense that something was wrong. I told him that I loved him and that I was there for him. No matter what he was going through or what was going on, I would be there for him and help him through it. He began to cry. I attempted to get him to open up to me but he wouldn't share anything with me. I left his room and went back to my room to get ready for work. Steve left for school and I was getting ready to leave for work. I picked up my phone to check my emails before I left the house. I had four text messages. I opened them to start reading. They were from a girl that Steve used to date. She told me that he had been using Cocaine, that she had been trying to help him and get him to stop, and that she was worried about a big party he was planning to go to that weekend. She was scared for him and wanted to tell me so I could help.

I was in shock. This must be the reason that I woke up in the middle of the night. God was sending me a message. I shivered at the thought and became incredibly emotional. I didn't know what to do or where to turn. I called my boss and told him that I had a family situation and I would not be in to work that day. I remembered a woman that I used to work with. Her son had been involved with drugs and she had successfully gotten him help. I called her. She gave me a number to call. I also called my church and got some resource numbers from them. I started calling places to find out about rehab or other resources that were available to me. Call after call resulted in nothing. Either the facilities did not accept minors or if they did, it was voluntary only and the cost was around $500 per day for a child to stay there. How could I possibly afford that? It was so devastating and I felt helpless.

My mind was racing. I had no idea what to do. I was so scared. I decided to call the school and speak with them. They were very supportive and said they would pull Steve into the office and speak with him. After they did that, they would call me and I would go to the school and meet with them and Steve. They called Steve into the office. He had just had an off hour the class before and when they looked at him, they thought he was high. The nurse took him to her office and did an examination. His eyes were dilated, his responses were delayed, and one of his nostrils was swollen indicating something had been snorted through it. Since Steve was high at school, they suspended him and required him to go to a drug and alcohol class.

Steve was furious with me. He denied the allegations about him using cocaine. He said his ex-girlfriend was lied. He thought I over reacted. I was certain that he was the one lying. I knew this in my head, but in my heart, I was so confused and had no idea what to do. Eventually I got him to admit he had been doing some drugs, but he still said he didn't have a problem, he was not an addict, and he could stop whenever he wanted to.

I had no idea how to navigate these waters. I had never been in any situation like this and didn't know anyone else who had. It felt like the system was not setup to really help people. Each place I turned pushed me away instead of pulling me in and providing the shelter, the help, the comfort, and the security that I needed. Even the school system did not provide the help I thought they would. Their primary concern was not helping me and my child but pushing the problem away from them. First by suspending my son, and then when he returned to school, they wanted the names of the drug dealers so they could also suspend them. When Steve refused to provide names, the school administration threatened us and forced Steve to withdraw from school with only three months left in his senior year. They said if he didn't withdraw, they would look for any little thing he did, and if he committed any violation of school policy, they would expel him and he would not be able to graduate. We had no choice but to withdraw. Fortunately, Steve had been an honor roll student and in AP classes throughout high school and only needed ½ of an English credit to graduate. He took a class online and was able to graduate with his class. In hindsight, I wish I had never involved the school. I am sure I made a ton of mistakes and should have done things very differently, but in the middle of a storm with no clear path and no compass to help you navigate, one ends up lost at sea, unable to see the beacon of light to guide the way.

The other avenues of help we explored didn't produce any better results. In the state of Colorado, the age of consent for mental health is 15. At the age of 15, a child can make their own decisions and can refuse to allow their parents to have access to any of their medical or mental health records. When we went to the mental health clinic, Steve decided not to allow me permission to see or hear about any of his records. I could not sit in on any therapy sessions, and I could not get any information about their assessment of him. I flip flopped back and forth wondering if he was really an addict or not. Did he really have a problem or was he just experimenting? Was I crazy or not? I couldn't even trust my own emotions. I am not even sure how to describe how I was feeling or what I was thinking. It was a time in my life that I would never wish on anyone else and a time that I never want to experience again.

This was just the start of more drama to come and I was not prepared for any of it. All I wanted was to help my child. I wanted to fix things but I had no idea how to do that. I felt so completely helpless. I had spent my entire life, from the time I was a small child, fixing things. I had always been successful solving problems and was not used to being in a situation where whatever I tried did not work. I talked and talked to Steve, I pleaded with him to stop, to seek help but nothing worked. I checked into various resources. I came to the conclusion that unless you are poor or rich, there is no help that is available. If a family has a lower income, there are free services that are available. If you can afford $500 a day to have your child in a facility, the help needed is at your disposal. However, if you are in the middle class and have some money but not an unlimited supply, good luck finding the resources that you need. It is so sad that our society has come to this. I know that these statements may not be completely fair and there are most likely some good resources out there, but they are hard to find. They are especially hard to find when the parent is in a mindset of desperation and can't seem to think straight. This is exactly why you cannot do this alone. It is why, I have given you the Sanity Savers and plead with you to seek help from professionals, your family, and friends in your support network. Let's look at some Sanity Savers to help you when you're feeling helpless:

Sanity Savers

Sanity Savers:

1. Find a Counselor
2. Gather Resources
3. Find a mentor for your Child
4. Join a Support Group

1. **Find a Counselor**

    ❖ Contact your physician or insurance company for a
       recommendation on a good therapist. You may also get
       a referral from friends or family. Some other
       alternatives are to go online and review profiles of
       potential therapists. Almost all therapists now have
       websites with their bios. Many will speak with you over
       the phone to understand your needs, tell you about
       themselves, and let you know if their specialties can
       help you with your situation. Ensure that you find
       someone that you are comfortable with. It may take
       some time to find the right therapist, so if you don't like
       the one you have chosen, don't give up. Keep looking
       until you find the right therapist.

2. **Gather a list of Resources**

    ❖ Begin to gather a list of resources, even if you don't
       need them now. A good place to start is with the deans
       at your high school. They will generally have a list of
       resources ranging from counselors to drug and alcohol
       classes, suicide hotlines, or other facilities and support
       groups. Ask your counselor or therapist for a list of
       various resources. Your physician can also be a good
       resource to direct you to the type of resource you
       currently need or may need in the future. Having a list
       at your fingertips is the best option because when you

are in crisis, you will not have the time, energy, or clear thinking to get what you need.

3. **Find a mentor for your child**
   ❖ It is important for your child to have someone that they can confide in besides their parent. It may be difficult for your child to talk to you about what is happening. If there is someone that your child looks up to, or someone that you think would be a good influence on them, encourage that relationship. I think this is especially important for boys if their father is not an active part of their life. A strong, responsible, respectable male may be the exact thing that your son needs to help them get through whatever it is they are going through.

4. **Join a Support Group**
   ❖ Support groups are a great place to find helpful resources. You will be with a group of people who are walking in your shoes, and who can share their experiences and feelings with people who have experienced some of the same issues and struggles. Not only can others help you but you may find you can help them as well. Hopefully the camaraderie that is created in support groups will give you the comfort and hope that you are looking for. Some support groups include Nar-Anon, Al-Anon, Autism, ADHD, and many other groups. Search the web to find groups in your area.

As you work through finding help for you and your child, keep in mind that you need to decide how much help you should give to your child. Sometimes, in our quest to help and protect our children, we can be enablers. Tough love is sometimes the best medicine. If we don't allow our children to feel the pain, they will never get to a point where they actually seek the help they need.

In one of the classes that I took, we watched a video that was incredibly insightful for me. The woman in the video explained the cycle of addiction in a way I had never heard before. This light bulb moment provided me with a new insight. The counselor began by asking us to write down answers to the following questions:

1. What does an alcoholic look like?

2. What does a drug addict look like?

She asked us to answer each question in detail. Take a minute right now to answer the questions too. Steve and I each wrote down our responses. Our responses included things like: homeless, dirty, carries around a brown bag, bad teeth, and crazy. Feel free to visual your thoughts of an alcoholic or addict. Now, here is how an addict thinks...they take that image which is part of their belief system that we are taught throughout our lives from a very young age and they say, "That is NOT what I look like". So in their minds, they aren't an addict. They deny that they have a problem and they continue down the same path that they are on. As the cycle continues, they begin to lose jobs, family, friends, car, etc. Without a job and no family support, they will actually, at some point, look like that alcoholic or addict they envisioned. At the point they have felt the pain and want it to stop, they will seek the help they need.

As parents, if we step in and prevent our loved ones from feeling that pain, it makes it that much harder for them to change or want to change. I know the strong desire that is within a parent to want to help our children, but until they are ready AND want the help, there is nothing that we can do. Unfortunately, most children will not learn from the wisdom or experience of their parents. They need to learn for themselves and sometimes that means learning the hard way.

6 WHAT'S GOING TO HAPPEN? (FEAR)

During my children's teenage years, I suffered a variety of different fears. It started with fears of them not graduating high school. I was afraid that if they didn't have a high school diploma, they wouldn't be able to get a good job and would struggle financially. I think my fear was driven by my own struggles as a young woman and new Mom. I wanted to spare my children from those same struggles so I became frantic that they had to finish high school. I think those are some of the same fears that every parent experiences. Those fears were very valid and real to me at the time, however, as my children began to act out in other ways, besides skipping classes and not doing homework, I realized how trivial those fears were. In the big scheme of things, not having a high school diploma is not the end of the world and is not a sentence of an unsuccessful life. A real fear is that my child wouldn't have any future if he ended up a drug addict that would not seek the help he needed. My fears created a sense of insecurity and a deep desire to protect my child and keep him safe. The problem with this mindset is that there is no way to completely protect your child. Maybe when they are infants, a parent can do that since they are 100% dependent. As they grow and become teenagers, they gain their independence and you can't be with them 24/7. They make their own choices and aren't always honest about where they are and what they are doing. I am sure that many of us would love to just lock them in the house and not allow them to leave, but that is not reality.

When we experience fear, the natural way to combat it is to take control. If we can control the situation, it will give us relief from the fear. When my son, Jay, was failing classes that he needed in order to graduate, I instinctively took control. I got online every day to see what homework had been assigned. I sat with him every night to make sure the homework got done. I checked to make sure he had turned it in. This was my way to ensure that he graduated. After all, what would happen if he didn't have a high school diploma? He won't be able to get a good job; he will struggle with finances and have a hard time making ends meet, and on and on and on. It is funny how our minds work and can take the smallest thing and think it is the end of the world. We make it so much bigger than it really is or has to be. Then there is the other extreme, when your child is using drugs and alcohol and is approaching the point of becoming an addict. That is a big deal and we are scared of what will happen to them. They won't listen to our advice; they won't seek help. So what do we do? We think, if he is in my home then I control what he does, who he hangs out with, where he goes. So we keep them in our house and we hide our medicine and throw out the alcohol. We ask them where they are going, who they are going to be with, and in extreme cases, we beg them to stay home. I remember telling my son, please, please don't go out. I am afraid of what will happen, I am afraid of what you will do. The thing that we need to remember is that NO ONE can change our child except them. The only one we have control over is ourselves and we can only change ourselves. No matter what we do or don't do, if the addict wants to get high or drunk or whatever it is they are doing, they will find a way. I bought a security box to lock-up my Ambien and other medications that I had around the house. I put my spare car keys in there. Do you think that stopped my son from getting them? I thought it did, but I was wrong. He picked the lock with a paper clip and got in. He was crushing and snorting my Ambien and taking my car when I carpooled to work. The point is, we cannot watch them 24/7, and we can't make the right choices for them. It is something they need to figure out on their own. As much as we want to help them and protect them, we are powerless to do so.

There are things that we can do though. We can set boundaries, we can strictly enforce the rules, and set clear limits. We can change ourselves and we can love them unconditionally so when they are ready to make the changes in their lives, they know we are there to love and support them. Until that happens, all we can do is hope and pray the day of recovery will come. When that day does come, we will look back on these times and be grateful that our children figured out life and we all survived the turmoil.

One Sunday afternoon, I got a phone call from a hospital. It was a nurse asking for permission to treat my son at the emergency room. I asked them what he was being treated for and they said they could not discuss it with me. Crazy, huh? You want my permission to treat him, because he is under 18, but you can't tell me what his injuries are? The nurse handed the phone to a guy named Shaun, who had taken Steve to the emergency room. I had no idea who this person was. It turns out he was the stepfather of a girl that Steve had started dating. He said Steve was getting an x-ray for his hand, which they thought was broken.

A couple of weeks before I got this phone call, Steve came home and asked if his girlfriend, Daisy could go with him to the drug and alcohol class we had been attending together instead of me. I wasn't crazy about the idea, but he convinced me it would be okay. I told him I wanted to see the receipt as proof he actually went to the class so I could be assured that he actually attended. Well, he left that evening and never came back home. He was living with this girl and her Mom. Daisy's Mom had been evicted from their home and they were staying with a relative in Denver. I was not happy with this arrangement, but I was also near a breaking point and no longer had much fight in me.

When I talked to this Shaun guy on the phone, I asked if he would bring Steve home as soon as they got done at the hospital. He was so nice and polite and said of course he would drop Steve off. He even wrote down our address. I had this gut feeling that I should just go down to the hospital myself, but I ignored it and convinced myself to wait for Shaun to drop off Steve. After 2 ½ hours, there was still no sign of my son. I was upset that I hadn't listened to my intuition and gone down to the hospital. I started talking to my husband about what we should do when the phone rang again. It was the doctor from the hospital. She said she called me because she was concerned about the situation with my son, Steve. She said that after she treated him and they left, she decided to check into his records further. The first thing that made her suspicious was that this guy, Shaun, was very adamant that Steve be given pain meds for his hand. She said Steve was not asking for the medication, but Shaun was, and he was very insistent. When she began to look through Steve's file, she found that he had been to another hospital earlier in the day for the same injury. In addition, Shaun had told her they needed the medication because they were getting ready to go to California as soon as Steve turned 18 which was in two days.

I was in a total panic. My heart was pounding, I was feeling sick to my stomach, and I was so scared that this person was going to take my son out of state. Who knows what would happen to him at that point. All I knew is that I needed to find my son and stop him from leaving Colorado. I couldn't believe that Steve was going from hospital to hospital to obtain pain pills. The thought of that made me sick. What had happened to him? Why was he doing this? I knew he needed help. I started calling around and somehow got an address for where Steve had been staying with Daisy and her Mom, Dee. My husband and I got in the car and headed over there. I called the police on the way and asked them to meet us there. I had no idea what we would find or how the situation would play out. My husband was worried that the situation could turn violent, and he didn't want anyone to get hurt.

When we arrived at the house, Steve's car was not there. We waited a little bit and the police still hadn't arrived. I couldn't wait any longer, I was so anxious to know what was going on and where my son was. I was hoping that, even though the car wasn't there, maybe he was. I got out of the car and went to the door. I knocked and a little boy answered the door. I asked to speak to a grown-up. A woman came to the door. I told her that I was Steve's mom and that I was looking for him. She said that she had kicked Shaun and Dee out the week before and she had no idea where they had gone. She said she told Steve that he could stay because she thought he was a good kid. Shaun and Dee had told her that I neglected and abused Steve and that was the reason he was staying with them. She proceeded to tell us that Shaun and Dee were both pill popping drug addicts. They had been living off of her for a couple of months. They weren't buying any groceries or helping with anything else around the house. Shaun had just gotten out of jail recently and all of them had been living in her basement because they had nowhere to go. Her husband had gotten Shaun a job at a construction supply company where he worked. They had been using Steve's car to get around because they had no other form of transportation. Steve had a job at the time at the local movie theater near our home and Shaun told Steve that he needed to quit the job because it was too far to drive. The real reason is that they wanted to use his car. They had also been using his cell phone and ran up an extensive bill for overage minutes.

At one point Shaun had threatened Steve because he thought something might be going on with Steve and Dee. Both Shaun and Dee were always desperate for the next high and would do anything to get it. The night before she kicked them out, they wanted to run over Daisy's hand with Steve's car to break it so they could take her to the hospital to get pills. I asked her if she thought he had broken Steve's hand. She didn't know. The police arrived, and I told them everything that she had shared with us. The police officer wondered if Steve was being held against his will and if it might be a kidnapping. The woman who owned the house did not think that was the case. The police said they could keep an eye out for Steve's car but there was nothing they could do beyond that.

I couldn't believe this was happening. The story we were told sounded more like a soap opera than real life. Did people actually live this way? I could never imagine, in my worst nightmares, that my child would be involved in situations like this. He was being hurt, or intentionally hurting himself, in order to get pain pills to get a high. I had no idea Daisy's parents were involved in this type of fraud and manipulation. It horrified me to know that Steve had been living with them under these circumstances.

I know there are many stories far worse than mine. No matter what the situation, it is still shocking for any parent to experience. The unknown, the uncertainty, and most of all the FEAR that grips you in a situation like this. You think, this is my baby. What has happened to him and what is going to happen to him now? I wanted to know where he was so desperately. I wanted to bring him home where I knew he would be safe. There was no way that I could go home and sleep that night.

Before we left the house, I asked as many questions as I could to find out where they might be or how to find them. We were able to get the address of where Shaun worked. My husband and I decided to get up early the next morning and stake out his employers so we could see if Steve dropped him off at work or get the car when Shaun showed up. We woke up at 4:00 am to drive across town and wait at the warehouse where he worked. We waited for an hour and a half, but he never showed up. It was disappointing, but I had another idea. Steve's birthday was coming up and we had a family tradition to go to the birthday person's favorite restaurant to celebrate. We had never missed a year. So even though Steve would not answer most of my calls, I knew he wouldn't want to miss his birthday celebration. Plus, he would assume I would give him money for his birthday, which I am sure he needed. I had already learned my lesson about giving him cash. I couldn't trust he wouldn't spend the money on drugs or alcohol. So, I said nothing about the call from the hospital or the trip to the house where they had been staying. I simply sent him a message that I wanted to take him to dinner for his birthday and asked if he could come over to the house and we would go out to eat. He happily agreed to this.

I was so excited! This was my chance to get him home and make sure that he stayed there this time. We planned to take the car away from him. Our thinking was, even if he didn't stay at our house, at least he wouldn't have a car to be driving around in and possibly hurt himself or others if he drove in a condition that was impaired. Hopefully, without his car, Shaun and Dee would lose interest in him.

The evening of Steve's birthday arrived and he showed up at our house with Daisy. I invited them inside. My husband went out the back door and around to Steve's car and removed the battery. When he came back in the house, we all got into our car and went out for dinner. We had a good evening and when we returned home, I told Steve that I wanted him to stay at the house. He said he couldn't. He needed to go back. I told him he could leave, but not with the car. He was furious. He said that I tricked him into coming home, which I had. What choice did I have? Steve said he was not staying, and they walked out of the house. As they were leaving, Steve punched the garage with his casted hand, leaving a big dent, and walked down the street. I think they ended up staying with some friends that night.

The next day, my husband and I started to clean out the car. The entire family had been living in Steve's car. There were clothes, food, mail, and a cast cutter in the car. I started going through items and found x-rays, doctor's notes, and even prescriptions for pain pills that had not been filled yet. Shaun had been taking Steve to different hospitals and even using different names to get x-rays and prescriptions for pain medication. Shaun had also sprained Daisy's wrist in order to get a prescription in her name for pain medication. As best we could tell, they had been getting Steve's hand x-rayed, casted at a hospital, then cut it off, and take him to another hospital to repeat the process. In the open mail we found in the car, there were letters from hospitals that Dee had gone to in order to get pain pills and the hospitals were investigating her for drug abuse and medical fraud.

You can only imagine the fear and disbelief that we were going through. First of all, I had no idea that people lived like this, at least no one that I knew. We are a middle class family with a Christian foundation. My child had been living in a car with these people and doing indescribable things. I couldn't understand how he got to this place and why he would want to stay in that situation rather than be in a loving home, with a warm bed, food, and clean clothes. The fear I felt for Steve was tremendous. I was scared for him, but I knew that until he was ready to seek help, there was nothing that I could do. I was afraid for his safety and well-being.

Even now, after all that I have been through, I still struggle with fear. When I haven't heard from my son in a while I get this sense of panic inside of me and my mind takes me to all kinds of crazy thoughts. I think, maybe he is using again. What if he is in trouble or has been arrested and that is why I haven't heard from him? Sometimes it is still a battle for me to not let fear get the better of me.

In times of deep fear, it is important to remember that you cannot let fear drive you and control the decisions that you make. If you do, you may make poor decisions that are driven by emotions and not driven by logic and what is best for your child in the long run. Be very careful not to enable your children which won't help them but will instead allow them to stay in the same place where they are. The ultimate goal is to get them to a better place.

Let's take a look at some sanity savers to help combat fear. I hope these will help you to release the fear and prevent it from taking hold of you.

Sanity Savers

> Sanity Savers:
>
> 1. Pray
> 2. Define your Fear
> 3. Change Negative Thinking into Positive Thinking
> 4. Release Control

1. Pray

❖ Prayer allows us to give our burdens to God and feel his peace. As it says in Matthew 11:28, "Then Jesus said, Come to me, all of you who are weary and carry heavy burdens, and I will give you rest."

❖ As we have talked about throughout the book, you cannot change your child, but God has the power to change anyone and anything. In James 5:16, it says "...The prayer of a righteous person is powerful and effective." Not only should you pray for your child, you should also ask others to pray for your child.

❖ Prayer can bring you wisdom. Read James 1:5. It says, "If any of you lacks wisdom, you should ask God, who gives generously to all without finding fault, and it will be given to you."

2. Define your Fear

❖ Take some time and think about what you fear the most. Is that fear realistic? What triggers it? If possible, avoid the things that trigger your fear. For example, as I mentioned, when I haven't talked to my son in a while, my thoughts can run wild. So I ask him to keep in touch with me on a regular basis so that I know he is doing okay and it prevents my fears from rising up and growing into monsters. How do your fears affect you? How can you overcome them? Make a plan so you can keep the fears at bay or prevent them altogether.

3. Change Negative Thinking into Positive Thinking

❖ When you have those negative or fearful thoughts, change them around to something more positive. In my example of imaging my son in jail or using again, instead of letting my mind go there, I needed to imagine a positive outcome. I have not heard from my son in a couple of days because he is busy with school and work and I am proud that he is staying busy rather than getting in trouble. Each time a negative thought comes into your mind, turn it around to a positive thought.

4. Release Control

❖ Release control of the fear. You cannot control it, and you cannot let is control you. Let it go. Stand up to it. Make a plan so that you have a way to escape it. Hand over your problem to God and let him carry the burden for you. Release the pressure that you feel and trust that in time, and by God's will, this too shall pass and in the end something good will come out of it!

7 IS THERE ANY HOPE?

I've never been a big fan of roller coasters. I get motion sickness and that is not usually a good combination with a roller coaster. Not only do I get motion sickness, but I find it frightening when the roller coaster goes through a tunnel of darkness where I can't see the next turn and don't know what is coming next. Some people find that very exciting. Me, I prefer to see where I am headed and know what is around the next bend. I guess that also makes me a bit of a control freak.

Life with my son, Steve, was just like a roller coaster ride that lasted for a couple of years. Steve would do something, get caught, and then promise to never do it again. His behavior changed for a week or two and then he was in trouble again. This went on month after month. We punished him by taking away privileges and possessions. As soon as he was no longer grounded, a new event would bring us back to the same place. It got to the point where everything had been taken away from him. No phone, no video games, no car, no allowance, no computer, and no TV. No matter what we did, it did absolutely nothing to change his behavior. It was frustrating, but worst of all, it felt like I was on an emotional rollercoaster that I couldn't get off. My husband, was tired of it and hated what it was doing to me. Things got so bad that he said Steve had to go. We had to kick him out of our house. Steve left our house and went to stay with a friend until his welcome there wore out or he got desperate for the comforts he had once enjoyed. At that point, he called and begged me to let him come back home. The conversation started with, "Please, Mom. Please. I will change! I won't do those things again. I will follow the rules. I don't have anywhere else to go! I am hungry! I have nothing to eat and no money." The begging, pleading, and apologies would go on and on until I gave in. I was worn down and so tired of the endless drama that defined our lives. I felt sorry for him, I loved him, and hoped that things would truly change this time. I argued with my husband, tried to convince him that we needed to give Steve another chance and let him come back home. This caused much strife between my husband and me. In fact, the divorce word came up on several occasions. My son, through his actions and my responses, was threatening my marriage. My husband is an incredible man who loves me very deeply, but it was extremely hard for him to see what Steve was putting me through. Steve's actions didn't just affect me. Steve treated my husband horribly, calling him names and even getting physical at times. Even with all of the ups and downs, we eventually gave him another chance and let him come home again. We established rules, typed them up into a contract, and even had Steve sign the contract agreeing to abide by the rules.

Obeying the rules would only last for a short time and then everything went back to how it was before. Steve lied to us, broke the rules, and eventually get caught. Steve was so sincere in his apologies and promises to change. I would gain hope that things would change and then those hopes were crushed, time and time again. It was that rollercoaster of up and down emotions that took its toll on me. I was emotionally drained. I had lost my fight. I was beginning to compromise. The line I mentioned in Chapter 1 just moved further and further away from the boundaries that we once had. I thought that maybe if I lightened up a little, gave him a little more freedom, then he would make the right choices. Harsh punishment didn't work and neither did giving him some freedom to make his own choices. I got to the point of being severely depressed. Would it ever change? Would

Steve ever change? I was losing hope, unable to see a way off the rollercoaster we were on.

When hope isn't there, we often feel sad, depressed, and have an overall negative perspective on things. It is hard to find that hope again and to feel positive about the future. I was in that place and I know how difficult it is. I felt beaten down, and every time I gained a little bit of hope, that hope was dashed by the latest crisis. It is hard to see past it and believe there will be a light at the end of the tunnel. Many people told me that my son would grow out of it and someday things would be better. I tried to hope for that, but it was difficult. I still struggle with it even though my son is doing better now. He still has set backs and I have to guard myself against feeling hopeless. Here are some Sanity Savers to practice to regain your hope:

Sanity Savers

Sanity Savers:

1. **Find a Friend or Mentor**
2. **See your Doctor about Anti-Depressants**
3. **Re-define Failure**
4. **Celebrate the small victories**

1. Find a Friend or Mentor

❖ Being around other people can help us to feel better. You realize that we are not alone and hanging out people will lift your spirits even though you may not feel like being around other people. A friend or mentor can help you see things that you may not be able to see because you are too close to the situation and aren't as objective. It is also a great hope to hear stories from others who have been there and have come through the other side. That will help you to believe there is hope in your situation too. Often we think our situation is unique but the more that you open up, you will find others who have had similar circumstances, and you will realize there are many people who have been exactly where you are. They survived and so will you!

2. See your Doctor about Anti-Depressants

❖ I do not think drugs are the answer for everything and, for most of my life, I have been opposed to seeking medication to help me overcome sadness or other feelings of despair. However, my life got to a point where I was physically and emotional damaged, and it was not something that a change of attitude was going to fix. Anti-depressants helped to alleviate the debilitating headaches that I experienced every day and helped me to function properly day by day. Consult with your doctor to find out if this is a good course of action for you.

3. Re-define Failure

❖ Success is achieving a desired outcome. Failure is the opposite of success, not achieving that desired outcome or objective. In life, there is not just one thing that makes us a success or failure. Life is a marathon and not a sprint. There are going to be plenty of times when we experience great achievements and other times when we experience defeats. In the road of life, there are many different paths to the same destination so don't let this period of time in your life define who you are or who your child is. Ralph Waldo Emerson said, "Our greatest glory is not in never failing, but in rising up every time we fail." I would actually change that just a little bit to say "but in rising up every time we **fall**". So, keep getting up, keep hoping, and one day you will look back on this time in your life and realize, it wasn't failure, but rather a journey, that made you a stronger and more compassionate person.

4. Celebrate the small victories

❖ When you are losing or have lost hope, it is easy to focus on the negative. Instead, look for the small victories and celebrate them. Did your child pass a test at school, get a good grade on homework, or come home before their curfew? Any little victory is a step in the right direction. We need to encourage that behavior and we ourselves need to cling to that little bit of hope and build on it. In Romans 12:9, it says "…Hate what is evil; cling to what is good.".

8 WHY IS THIS HAPPENING?

Do you know what the chances of winning the lottery are? It is about 1 in 175 million. Winning a second time, the chances are 1 in billions and winning the same lottery, with the same numbers, is 1 in 5.2 trillion. Guess what? It has happened; not once but multiple times to many different people. Why is that? Why are some people so lucky and others can't seem to catch a break? It seems a little unfair. I used to believe that things happened to people because of the choices that they made. If they didn't make good choices, then the consequences were not good. I based this belief on some of my experiences growing up and on stories I heard. Stories like kids growing up with parents that were neglectful or families being homeless and their children working really hard to change their circumstances, growing up to be successful, regardless of where they started. I thought the way you overcome anything in life was just to work hard and stay positive. In the book, <u>The Secret</u> (Rhonda Byrne, 2006), the secret to success is based on the premise there is a law of attraction in the universe. Good things come to those that believe it will happen and stay positive. It brings negative things to those who think negatively. This sounds over simplistic, doesn't it? Look at it in terms of a cancer diagnosis. Cancer doesn't play favorites. It doesn't care what you look like, your outlook on life, your economic status, or anything else. It is random and hits whenever and wherever it wants. We have no idea why some people suffer and others seem to have things come so easily for them.

I have always lived my life avoiding the question "Why?" I know so many people who question why things happen, why God allowed it. I guess I have always had a healthy fear of God and trust that if he has allowed something to happen then there must be a reason for that and it is not mine to question. However, after struggling through the teenage years with both of my children, I found myself no longer able to sit back and trust. I began to ask, "Why?"

As you have read in the other chapters of this book, I had been through a lot of challenges with both of the boys. When Jay was a teenager and started to act out, I became stressed and found myself feeling a lot of guilt. I was still trying to deal with that when Steve started acting out. What I found myself dealing with from Steve's actions was something that I could never have imagined. I thought at the time that Jay's teenage years were tough but they were nothing compared to Steve's teen years. As a parent, I thought I had done everything right. I loved my kids. I spent a lot of time with them. They played sports, they had childhood friends, they had a good Christian foundation, they were loved, and they were taught right from wrong. I had taught them valuable life lessons. I set a good example for them with my actions. So, I found myself asking, "Why?" Why was this happening? Why had my children turned out like this? Why was I being punished?

I had grown up in a single parent household, and we didn't have very much. I knew early on in life that I wanted to provide more for my own kids and be able to give them things that I never had. I worked hard to provide for them. I wanted my kids to have a good life, a normal life. Where I found myself was anything but normal. I would be at work, or other social settings, and hear people talking about their kids and how they were planning to go to college and study this or that. I would hear about how well they were doing in school or what clubs or sports they were involved in. It was painful to hear those stories when I knew that I wanted those same things for my children, but for some reason it was not turning out that way. Again, the question, why?

Most of the time we will never have the answer to our why. Some people never get to see their children grow up because of some tragedy like an accident or disease that takes their life. Those people will never know why their child was chosen and not someone else's. Only God knows and we will not know the answer to why until we get to heaven and can ask God. Sometimes, in hindsight, you can see that the tragedy helped to shape the character of those parents or their child. It gave them an opportunity to use the experience to be a better person or help others. I think that is the answer to my why. I had a very difficult period in my life for a little over 5 years. I do not believe that my experiences were in vain; I believe God allowed it to change my character and to allow me the opportunity to help other people. As I mentioned in previous chapters, I was a critical and judgmental person. I thought life was a formula, and if you followed the formula, things turned out the way that they should. Boy was I wrong!

I spent a good year or more questioning why my children had gone through these experiences and why it affected me so much to the point of making me physically and emotionally sick. What had I done? What hadn't I done? Why? The conclusion I came to was that I can't control life. I can't control my own and certainly cannot control the life of my boys. Sometimes there is just no one to blame. Sometimes things just happen. Sometimes we need to stop asking why and just accept things for what they are. It will tear you up inside if you focus on what should be or what shouldn't be. Accept things as they are. That doesn't mean that you stop fighting or stop hoping. You need to continue fighting for your children, but don't drive yourself crazy wondering what happened or what you should have done. You will never find peace if you continue to ask "Why?" It is now time for your child to accept responsibility for their actions and determine if and how they want to change their lives.

You will need to dig deep and find faith to trust that God will work for the good in your situation. Trust that this storm will not last forever.

Trust that your child will grow, mature, and begin to understand what they are doing to their lives. They will get tired of the mess they have created and eventually realize they need to do something differently. Until that time comes, you need to focus on getting and staying healthy so you can be the person that you were meant to be and not allow these circumstances to define who you are and how you feel. I know it is not easy, but keep putting these sanity savers into practice, stay positive, and you too will find freedom and happiness again. It is no fun being trapped by fear, worry, depression, and stress. We were not created for that and no one wants that to define their life. Here are some more suggestions to help you.

Sanity Savers

> Sanity Savers:
>
> 1. **Trust God**
> 2. **Find Acceptance**
> 3. **Don't compare yourself to others**
> 4. **Help someone else**

1. Trust God

- ❖ This sounds like such an easy thing to say and yet such a hard thing to achieve. When we don't know what the future holds it makes it difficult to blindly trust that things will work out for the good. God tells us that He works for the good in all things (Romans 8:28).

- ❖ God does not decide that we should go through difficult times. He does not want us to suffer. It is through our free will that we choose the path that we take. In our case, it is the path that our children or loved ones have taken that is affecting us. No matter what path our children take, God still works for the good and make the best of that situation. These situations, although unpleasant, will help us to develop a deeper character and grow in ways we wouldn't have, if we had not experienced these things. It does the same for our children.

2. Find Acceptance

❖ Finding acceptance is a way for you to find peace and be able to move forward. It does not mean that you are "Ok" with what has happened, or is happening. It simply means that you are no longer stuck in a place where you are constantly focused on why these things have happened. Instead you are ready to acknowledge where you and/or your children are, and you are ready to make plans to move to the next stage. Hopefully that step is making a plan to correct their situation, but sometimes that is out of your control.

❖ Find acceptance so you can invest in yourself again. This is the first step in the healing process.

3. Don't Compare Yourself to Others

❖ Stay away from comparing yourself to other people, other families, or other parents. Believe me, you have no idea what is going on with other people. They may look like they have it all together on the outside, but it could be completely different on the inside. No one is perfect and we all have some type of issue that we are going through.

❖ It is not healthy to compare yourself to someone else. It won't change anything and it certainly will not make you feel better. If you want to compare yourself to someone else, then look at examples of situations that are worse than yours. For example, in my situation at least my son didn't commit suicide or die of a drug overdose. I don't live in a third world country where there are no resources to help me. It can always be worse, and I need to count my blessings that it isn't.

4. Help Someone Else

❖ Don't let what you have gone through be in vain. Share your experiences with someone and give them the hope to get through what they are going through. Your answer to the Why may be to help someone else. The saying, "It takes a village to raise a child" is so true. We cannot, and should not, have to do it alone. Your experiences, when shared, can be a godsend to someone else who is struggling.

❖ 2 Corinthians 1:4 says, "He [God] comes alongside us when we go through hard times, and before you know it, he brings us alongside someone else who is going through hard times so that we can be there for that person just as God was there for us." MSG.

9 BROKEN DREAMS

When I look back at all of the things that I have been through and think of what has been the most difficult and hardest to overcome, broken dreams is that thing. I had high hopes and dreams of what my life, and the lives of my children, would be like. I had done well in school and graduated with honors. I got accepted to college but didn't have any money to pay for it. My mom had no means to borrow money to help me. I got a student loan, but it was a struggle, and I ended up dropping out of college after my freshman year to join the Army. I never gave up the dream of getting a college degree and went back to school when my boys were 2 and 5 while working full time. It was a difficult path to get my degree. I vowed to myself that my children would not have to suffer in that same way. I wanted them to go to college and I saved my money so that I could help them to do just that.

I envisioned my boys playing sports in high school, going to college, and getting good jobs after they finished school. They would not have to start at the bottom, as I did, and work their way up, struggling to make ends meet until they reached their goals. I know starting out at the bottom and working your way up is not a bad thing. It develops character and provides experiences that wouldn't be possible without following that path. I simply wanted life to be easier for my kids than it was for me.

Jay didn't want to go to college after high school. I was a little disappointed, but he has a good head on his shoulders. He works hard and has his own apartment. He is very independent and doesn't ask for any help. Steve had dreams of going to college, getting his degree and becoming an officer in the Air Force. He was working hard in school and was filling out an application for an Air Force ROTC scholarship. I was so proud. I wanted him to have the full experience of college. He would do well in school, make life-long friends, and have a nice career in the military. He applied to CSU (Colorado State University) and was accepted right away. He was on the path to success and I couldn't be happier.

Then things started to change. Steve started smoking pot. He wasn't very good at covering his tracks and was easily caught. I talked to him about his choices and so did his dad. We stressed the importance of making the right choices so he would not jeopardize his military aspirations. Not long after these conversations, I started noticing alcohol missing from the cabinet. I believe he continued to smoke pot on a regular basis and had been caught on several different occasions. He was also drinking, and then he began to crush and snort pills. I remember the first time that I caught him. I had gone upstairs to check on him and when I opened the door to his room, he quickly hid something under his leg. He was hoping that I didn't notice. I asked what it was, and he refused to tell me. I tried to grab it, and he got up and ran to the bathroom. He locked the door and flushed it down the toilet. I thought it was marijuana and he agreed and said, "Yeah, it was marijuana." I checked the baggy that he had thrown in the trash and realized that it was not marijuana. It was pain pills. He told me that someone at school had given it to him, and it was the first time he was trying it. He was telling me exactly what I wanted to hear. Over the next year or so, things continued to escalate. Steve was snorting pain pills, Ambien, Benadryl, cocaine and probably anything else that he could get his hands on. With the drugs came changes in his behavior.

School was no longer important. The future was something he was not even thinking about. Lying was second nature. He was often angry and acted out violently at times.

All of this slowly, and totally, destroyed me. It is like watching a sick person slowly dying right in front of your eyes. I did anything and everything that I could to stop it. Unfortunately, I was not successful.

The pain that this caused is something I am not sure I can even explain. My heart ached. It felt as though my heart was being ripped out of my chest. The hopes and dreams that I had for Steve, and that he had for himself, were slipping away. His GPA was dropping, and his opportunity to go to college was becoming less and less probable. I was afraid that even if he could still get into college that it would not be a good atmosphere for him. It would only give him more opportunities to use drugs and alcohol. Steve continued to let his life spiral out of control. He barely finished the required classes in order to graduate high school. The drugs and alcohol got him in trouble with the law. He got a DUI when he was 17. He was arrested and charged with drug possession and resisting arrest at 18. He violated his parole with alcohol and ended up in jail for a second time. Steve was a smart kid. What was he doing? No matter what happened or what I did to dissuade his behavior, nothing got through to him.

It broke my heart to see what he was doing with his life. He was not only hurting himself, but he was hurting me. I felt responsible, but most of all I felt sad. I was sad for both of us. I was sad for myself because I had wanted to see my child do well in life and be successful. I wanted to be the proud mom. I wanted him to have the kind of deep friendships that I had envied in other people. I knew people who went to college and made great friends that turned into life-long relationships. I never had the opportunity for that, and I wanted Steve to have it. I wanted him to have all of the things that I never could because I was not given those opportunities. Steve had the chance to have those experiences, but he was slapping the opportunity in the face and turning his back on it. It hurt to see those opportunities being so carelessly thrown away for the short-term pleasures of drugs and alcohol. I had spent my life working really hard so I could provide my kids with a great life. I was beginning to feel it was all for nothing.

I was also heartbroken to see how he had changed. When Steve was young, he was so full of life. He was charismatic. People loved to be around him and his smile and laugh would light up a room. He was so energetic and ambitious. He used to dream of different ideas for inventions and share them with me. Some of the ideas were already invented, but for the ones that weren't, he wrote them down in a notebook so one day he could create them. He was interested in how things worked and wanted to be smart about his future. He started saving all of the money he got for birthdays and holidays. When he got $500, he bought his first CD (Certificate of Deposit) at the age of 10. When I look at him now, most of those qualities are gone. He is no longer motivated. Some days, he doesn't even get out of bed. He can't budget his money and doesn't save a dime. In fact, the opposite is true. He spends money as fast as he gets it and then calls me to "loan" him money. When I talk to him about budgeting and saving money, he tells me, "I know Mom! I am not stupid!" However, he continues to do the same thing over and over again. When I refuse to keep "loaning" him money, he goes on a tirade and says really mean things to me. Like, I am the selfish one, I don't care about him, I have money, but won't help him. It breaks my heart time and time again. He is so far from the child that I knew and the person that I thought he would become. How can someone not feel bad or guilty when someone has changed so drastically? The person that he was is gone, and the person that he is now is not someone that I like very much. I don't know if it will ever change. I hope and pray that it will. Only time will tell.

So what do you do with a broken heart and broken dreams? How does one heal from that? I am not sure that I know the answer to those questions. The only answer that I have come up with is that you must accept a person for where they are and who they are. You can't make anyone be the person that you want them to be. You must decide every day to love, or not love, that person regardless of who or what they are. I can also tell you to not give up hope. I am sure that each of us can look back upon our lives and remember things we did that we wish we could take back and do over. There are mistakes that we have made. No one is perfect. Each of us has our share of screw ups. It is what we do with those mistakes that makes us the people that we have become. That is what keeps me hopeful. I have a new dream. My dream is that my son will learn from these things and as he matures, he will make better choices and one day will be a good man. He will be able to look himself in the mirror and be proud of the person that he has become. I will be proud too.

If you are struggling with broken dreams or a broken heart, here are some sanity savers that may help:

Sanity Savers

Sanity Savers:
1. Allow yourself to Mourn
2. Let go of Hurts
3. Find new dreams

1. Allow yourself to Mourn

❖ It is okay to mourn. You have lost something that is dear to you. It is no different than a death. I lost the son that I thought I would have. I still have a son, but he has changed and I miss the person that he used to be. Allow yourself to feel sad and take time to grieve. Once you have done that, it will be easier for you to let go and move on.

2. Let go of Hurts

❖ You will have a difficult time looking toward the future if you are stuck in the past. It is important to let go of the past, let go of the hurt that you feel, and forgive if you need to. If we don't let those feelings go, we will be trapped in a place that won't bring us happiness. I know it is hard to do that when you have been deeply hurt. Trust me, it takes so much more energy to keep that hurt and broken heart alive, than it does to let it go. So let go of the hurt and focus your energy on being happy and healthy. It is only then that you can look to the future and find new dreams that will bring you hope and happiness.

3. Find new Dreams

❖ The things that you hoped for and the dreams you had did not come true. Say good-bye to those dreams, mourn them if you need to, and then find new dreams. My new dream for my son is not college, a great job, and a successful military career. My new dream is that he will be healthy and happy. Most of all I want him to be happy. It may sound like a simple dream, but it is a good place to start. We all can use happiness.

❖ Find a new dream for you. Find a new dream for your child. Just start dreaming again. Don't let despair and hopelessness win. We lose only when we stop trying...so keep dreaming.

10 LET GO AND LET GOD

You've been on a journey that has led you through many different challenges and emotions. You have been stressed, worried, fearful, hopeless, and heart broken. You have done everything within your power to improve or fix the situations. So what do you do now? I am here to tell you that you have done all that you can. It is no longer your job, or mine, to attempt to control the lives of our children. My son is no longer a child. He is making his own decisions and I no longer have control over what he does or doesn't do. The more that I try to control the situations, the more frustrated I become.

I have gone through many ups and downs. There are times when I decide to "give up" and not get involved and then a week later, I turn around and try again to make a difference somehow and attempt to "fix" my son. It doesn't produce the results that I am looking for and he has learned that the best way to get me off his back is to tell me exactly what I want to hear. He promises to change, promises to do the right thing, promises to make the right decision, or whatever it is that I am asking him to improve. He is tired of me "hassling" him, and I am tired of watching him make the same mistakes over and over again.

So you may be asking yourself, "Then what do I do?" As long as you have a clear conscience that you have made every effort within your power to help your child, it is time for you to step back and let go. It is important to let your child know that you will always love them and be there for them when they are ready to change or ask for the help that they need. Beyond that, it is time for you to let your child make their own decisions, make their own mistakes, and deal with whatever consequences come along with those choices. Stop enabling your child. You cannot protect them from the choices that they are making and the more that you support them, the longer it will take for them to alter their behavior. Stop beating yourself up or beating your head against the same wall. Let go and let God watch over your child. Trust that God will be with them. He will watch over them and hopefully one day our child will see the light and begin to repair or rebuild their life. Hopefully they will turn to God and receive His love and grace. You just need to try not to worry, stay faithful, and one day, with God's grace, your child will find his way. The events of his life are shaping his character and he will become the person that God created him to be.

I know it is extremely difficult to not worry. I know that I still worry, and I am sure that I always will in some way or another. Instead of driving yourself crazy with worry, pray earnestly for your child. Pray that they will be safe, pray they will find the right path, pray they will meet someone who will influence them in a positive way. Pray they will turn to God.

Once you let go you will be able to begin the recovery process. You will start to feel more relaxed and be able to regain some happiness again. You will be able to focus on something other than the problem that has been at the forefront of your mind and life for so long. As you distance yourself from the situation, you will find that you are able to think more clearly. You will be able to regain your strength and get some much needed rest. You may also be surprised to see changes happening with your child as well. Once they realize that you aren't going to be there every second, of every day, for their every whim, they start to think before they act. They realize that you may not be there to bail them out and they begin to take responsibility for their actions. It can be a freeing experience for everyone.

Sanity Savers

Sanity Savers:

1. Divorce yourself from situations
2. Stop Enabling
3. Pray

1. Divorce yourself from situations

❖ Stop feeling like you need to be in the middle of the turmoil that is going on. You didn't create the situation and you don't need to fix it. Sometimes the best thing to do is step back, let things run their course and see what happens.

❖ It is so much easier to get perspective on a situation when you are looking at it from a distance. You are able to think more clearly and make better decisions.

❖ Sometimes the best way to protect yourself is to remove yourself from the situation. You need to decide if you are at the point where you can no longer take the drama. If that is the case, let your child know that you don't want to know what they are doing, you don't want to get pulled into the situation, and you want them to handle things on their own. It is like when kids are little and they fight with each other. Sometimes you tell them to work it out between themselves instead of you being the referee.

2. Stop Enabling your Child

❖ Don't be afraid to say "No". It doesn't mean that you don't love your child. It doesn't mean that you don't want to help. It simply means that I am not going to get involved in trying to solve the problem that you created.

❖ When we enable, we are taking away the consequences. If someone is never allowed to feel the pain of the choices they have made, they will continue to make those same bad choices. Let your child stay in jail; don't bail them out. Let your child experience what it feels like to be hungry, they will learn to budget their money better. Let them fail a class and have to take it again or go to summer school, they will learn to put in more effort next time.

❖ When you stop enabling, you free yourself from accepting responsibility for a problem that is not yours, one that you didn't create, and one that is not your responsibility to fix. You will feel better when you let go.

3. Pray

❖ You may not be able to fix the problem but God can. Nothing is impossible with God. Pray. It is a great way for you to let go and let God move in the situation. There are many paths to the same destination. Things could end up turning out better than you ever imagined or dreamed.

❖ Prayer is a great outlook to help you let go of the worry that you are experiencing every day. Prayer is a powerful tool. God wants to answer our prayers and He can influence situations and people.

❖ Don't be afraid to ask others to pray for you and children. Miracles can happen!

11 THE ROAD TO RECOVERY

It is time to take care of you. This chapter will focus on your personal recovery as the parent. Hopefully you have already begun your recovery as you have practiced the Sanity Savers. You should be learning to dream again. You have let go and are allowing your child, and God, to take control. You have been through difficult times and you are tired. Everyone deals with stress differently and that stress may have caused you to become depressed, caused you to turn to alcohol, smoking, food, or some other outlet that ultimately is not good for you. You deserve to be healthy and happy. It is time to focus on your recovery.

If you have developed any bad habits as you have dealt with the difficult situations in your life, you may need to take some time to break those habits. Start replacing those bad things with good things. Focus on getting healthy. That may include starting to eat right, exercising, and taking time to learn or practice relaxation techniques. Ask your friends or family to help you do whatever it is that you need to do in order to get healthy again. Find a partner to go to the gym with you. Get an accountability partner to help you eat right. Start going to church again if that is something you used to do and have stopped going. Take a good look at your life and see what it is that you need to change. You may not need to change anything and instead may just need to focus on letting go of the stress and finding joy again. Find something that you enjoy doing and DO IT. Don't make excuses, just make it happen.

Take time to relax. Go to a spa or get a massage. Take a long weekend or a vacation. Spend a day pampering yourself. You deserve a break and you should take it. Free up your schedule or reduce the number of activities that you have in your daily schedule. It will do you so much good to slow down just a little bit and take the time you need to feel better and stronger. You are not going to feel better overnight but you can get there fairly quickly if you focus on yourself. Find time to focus on simplifying your life and finding joy and relaxation again.

Start to laugh again. Go on a date night to a comedy club. You may have heard the saying that "laughter is the best medicine". Laughter is a great tool to help you feel better. Have friends over for a fun evening or have a night out with your friends. Just laugh! Watch a funny movie or find something that will bring some laughter to your life.

As you begin to work towards your recovery, ensure that you are getting enough sleep. Sleep is an important part to your recovery process. If you are like me, you will have experienced difficulty with your sleep patterns. If you have not already sought help for your sleeping, you may want to speak to your doctor and get a sleep aid. Other ways to improve your sleep patterns is to go to bed and get up at the same time every day. Don't stimulate your mind with video games, TV, computer, phone, or any other thing that gets your mind running. Instead take some time to relax before bed so that you are relaxed when you lay down and can quickly fall asleep. Once you start sleeping better, everything else will fall into place.

So far, I have talked about practical ways to start your recovery process. These will help you to physically heal, but you may also need to heal emotionally. The situations and experiences that have happened in my life, and the lives of my family, have profoundly affected me. I am not the same person that I used to be. In some ways, I am a better person. I am less critical and judgmental. I have more compassion for other people and the situations they are going through. Those are good

73

things, and I am grateful for those lessons that I have learned and the new person that I have become. On the flip side, these circumstances have changed me in ways that I didn't want and don't like. I lost the confidence that I once had. My self-esteem is lower, and I don't believe in my abilities the way that I used to. I was the type of person that believed nothing was impossible if you just worked hard enough, and now, that is gone. I am more fearful than I used to be. I have lost a piece of myself that I don't know if I will ever get back. It is okay to mourn that loss, but I can't dwell on it. I need to move on and learn to love the new person that I have become. My hope for you is that you will be able to do the same.

During my recovery period, I had the same dream on several different nights. In the dream, I was in a school building and I couldn't find my way out. I was scared and I kept running through the maze of halls and rooms trying to find the way out. Wherever I turned, there was something in my path or some frightening things that made me turn and run the other way. Sometimes, there was someone in the dream with me, and I would get separated from them. It made me so scared to feel alone. I looked for my companion and for the way out, but never found it. Then I woke up. My therapist asked me what I thought the dream meant. I told her that I thought it was symbolic of the things that I had been through and that I just felt like there was no end and no escaping it no matter how hard I tried. She then asked me to finish the dream. How would I get out of the building? I described the things that I would do, like look for exit signs or ask someone to help guide me out. Then she asked me, what I might find on the other side once I got out. I had never thought about that before. I came to realize that my dream was a metaphor for the life I had been living. I felt trapped in this emotional roller coaster where one bad thing after another kept happening and I didn't know what to do or where to turn. Finding the exit was only the beginning. I needed to plan for what was awaiting me on the other side. What kind of person did I want to be? Was I going to be crippled by what I had been through or was I going to become a new and better person? Once I stopped fighting, stopped trying to control the situations, and stopped being dragged into the drama, what was left for me to do? Where should I focus my attention? Could I really get off the roller coaster and find a new path for my life? The answer is yes!

What is on the other side of your exit sign? What will you find when you walk through that door? It is time for you to open new doors and write the next chapter of your life. That is what I must do and that is what you must do. This time in our lives will not define us and they are not the end of our story. We must recover from this time in our lives and explore the unlimited possibilities that the future holds for us. You are a wonderful and amazing person. You are smart and capable. You are ready to experience a full, happy, and healthy life. Start today by opening that door and seeing the endless possibilities.

Sanity Savers

Sanity Savers:

1. **Live YOUR Life**
2. **Find Joy**
3. **Stay Positive**
4. **Read <u>Feeling Good</u>**

1. Live YOUR Life

❖ It is time for you to put your time and energy into living YOUR life. Do what that you have been putting off. Do what you used to do or the things that you WANT to do. Find the things that are important to you and do those things. Stop living in crisis mode and just start living.

2. Find Joy

❖ What do you enjoy doing? Rekindle that love you had for the fun things in life. Maybe it is reading, doing crafts, game night, a night out with friends, special time with family, hiking, biking, whatever it is...start doing it again.

❖ Make a decision to be happy. Don't let things get you down. Surround yourself with people that are happy and love to smile. Joy is contagious.

3. Stay Positive

❖ Don't dwell on what has happened or what could have been, but instead focus on the positive. Nothing stays the same forever and things will get better. If you remain positive and look for those small victories, you will begin to feel stronger and find it easier to be positive and happy. You will grow healthier with each passing day.

4. Read **Feeling Good** (Burns, 2000)

❖ This book is a great resource to help you improve your mood and deal with depression without drugs. Dr. David D. Burns will help you to nip negative feelings, deal with guilt, improve your self-esteem and feel good.

12 REBUILDING

I live in Colorado and every summer and fall we have wildfires that affect our state. The wildfires destroy everything in their path, leaving nothing but bare tree trunks and charred debris and ash. For families that lose their home, it is devastating. All of the memories and symbols of the life they had are gone. All that is left is burnt up debris. What they have known and loved is now gone and they must start their lives again. This is the best analogy that I can think of to describe the rebuilding process of a relationship that has been destroyed by stress, chaos, and devastation.

The memories I have of how my children used to be, and the vision I had for their future are gone. I must accept the things that have happened and the way it has change my children and I. The personalities of all of us have changed and we must start anew. I must see them for what and where they are now. The memories of what we had before the destruction are physically gone and only live in my mind. What lies ahead is what I choose to make it. I can continue to mourn what could have been, or I can pick up the pieces of what is left and rebuild. In some cases you might be able to rebuild on the same site and foundation that you had before and in other cases, you must begin by building a new foundation. It may be very different from your previous home or life.

Tragedy changes us and there is no going back to the way it was before.

It is time to build a new foundation, determine what works now. Discover where it is you want to go on the new journey that you will build. If you are lucky, the storm will have truly passed and a new spring of life has been found. Your child has learned from what they have been through, from what they have put you through, and they are ready to start a new path that is less destructive and provides hope and change. If you are not so lucky, then you are at a crossroads where you have decided that your life must separate from that of your children (who are now young adults) or you must find what parts of your life will involve your child and what this renewed relationship will look like.

I have heard and read about families that have been broken so badly that the hope of rebuilding is lost...at least for a very long time. I have heard from other parents that they needed to sever the relationship in order to protect themselves. I have never been able to do that with my children. At times I have wanted to, but the distance didn't last much more than a week or two. Family is so important to me that I could never imagine not having a relationship with those I love. Additionally, my bond of love is so strong, I can't imagine anything breaking it. Not everyone is like me, and I understand that. Each of us must individually determine the path that we choose. My husband ended a relationship with his mother, and it was never repaired. She passed and he was completely unaware until he heard about it from a family friend. He has was hurt so badly by the relationship that he has no regrets that it was never rebuilt or repaired.

What I can tell you is that if your heart is open, and you are willing to forgive, you can move past the pain and hurt but you have to decide that is what you want. It is never easy and anything in life worth having is not always easy. It is a daily choice to love, a daily choice to be vulnerable, to allow your heart to be open knowing there is a possibility for more hurt. Keep hoping, keep praying, keep taking those steps day by day to repair and rebuild in the hope that one day it will be great again.

My hope is that, as you have read these words and practiced the sanity savers, you have found healing for your wounds. It takes time to heal, so take all of the time that you need. Seek the help you need for as long as you need it. Be open and honest with yourself and those around you. These are the things that will allow you to rebuild. Don't be sad for what you have lost, but instead, look forward and strive for what you can become. Your experiences were not for nothing. You can help others, you can become whatever it is that you choose to be. You have gained incredible wisdom and understanding.

I know for me personally, before my experiences, I was the person who judged. I was the person who said, Where are their parents and why didn't they raise their kid right? Now, I am the person who defends and gives the benefit of the doubt. I am the person who says, "I have been there, how can I help?"

The first thing you must do is focus on yourself and make sure that you are strong again. Focus on getting healthy. Once you have achieved that, you can bridge the gap between you and your child. Hopefully they have overcome their demons and are in a good place as well. If they aren't, then you can let them know that you will be there to support them when they are ready. Let them know that you will not support their bad decisions or continue to enable them, but you do love them and will get them the help they need. That help will most likely be a combination of help from you and other professionals.

Here are some final sanity savers for rebuilding those relationships when the time is right:

Sanity Savers

> Sanity Savers:
> 1. Accept your child for who and where they are
> 2. Plan Monthly Activities
> 3. Take a Family Vacation

1. Accept your Child for Who they are and Where they Are

❖ Let your child live their life. You cannot control what they do, when they do it, or how they do it. They may not be living the life we want them to live, but we can choose to love them. Love them right where they are at. You can still pray for them to get better or do better but accept them and love them now. You don't have to wait for them to change. Hopefully they will, but they may never change.

2. Plan Re-Building Activities once a month

❖ If you are ready to re-build your relationship, plan fun activities where you can hang out and just have fun with no drama and no strings attached. Go to a ball game. Go to a movie. Have a family game night. Do whatever it is that each of you likes to do. Plan something at least once per month, and over time, you will begin to feel that closeness again and you will be building new memories together that will keep you moving forward and continuing to heal.

3. Take a Family Vacation

❖ If you have the time, and the means to take a vacation, do it! We recently went on a family vacation and had the best time. It was the start of regaining that family closeness that we once had, and it created some great memories for us. Time is short and we never know what tomorrow will bring, so seize the moment and make the most of it!

RESOURCES

Nar-Anon Family Groups
Nar-Anon members are relatives and friends who are concerned about the addiction or drug problem of another.
www.nar-anon.org

Al-Anon Family Groups
Friends and families of problem drinkers find understanding and support at **Al-Anon** meetings.
www.al-anon.org

Find a Therapist
Site to assist in finding a therapist in your area.
www.find-a-therapist.com

Behavioral Health Treatment Services Locator
Help with drug, narcotic and other substance abuse and addiction problems, mental health problems, or other behavioral health issues.
find**treatment**.samhsa.gov

Family Support Meetup Groups
Helps **groups** of people with shared interests plan meetings and form offline clubs in local communities around the world about **Family Support**
family-support.meetup.com

CPSIA information can be obtained at www.ICGtesting.com
Printed in the USA
LVOW08s0352260214

375115LV00002B/18/P